SUMMER FLOODS 2007

Worcestershire Under Water

Kevin Ward

COUNTRYSIDE BOOKS
in association with
Worcester News

First published 2007
© Kevin Ward, Worcester News, 2007

COUNTRYSIDE BOOKS
3 Catherine Road
Newbury, Berkshire

in association with
WORCESTER NEWS

To view the full range of titles
from Countryside Books
please visit us at
www.countrysidebooks.co.uk

ISBN 978 1 84674 096 1

Designed by Peter Davies
Produced through MRM Associates Ltd., Reading
Printed by Cambridge University Press

All material for the manufacture of this book
was sourced from sustainable forests

INTRODUCTION

IT WAS the worst summer flooding in living memory.

Worcestershire is a county used to dealing with floods and their aftermath. But the scenes in June and July 2007 were something different. Nothing like them had been seen for more than 40 years.

Schools were evacuated, thousands stranded on motorways, hundreds of homes and businesses were devastated – and all at a time when we should have been soaking up the sun.

Staff at the *Worcester News* told the story of the floods in a series of dramatic reports and pictures during June and July. We, at the newspaper, were not immune to what was going on. Our own offices on Hylton Road in Worcester came within a few centimetres of being flooded – an event that would have been catastrophic for our business.

We were lucky – but so many of our readers were not. The *Worcester News* was there for them, reporting on the situation and providing help, advice and information. Our parent company Gannett donated £10,000 to the National Floods Fund to help those worst affected.

This book pulls together some of the most dramatic reports and pictures of the time. It is, I hope, the definitive account in words and pictures of the summer floods of 2007 as Worcestershire found itself under water.

Kevin Ward
Editor
Worcester News

ACKNOWLEDGEMENTS

The photographs contained in this book are the work of members of the team of photographers and reporters at *Worcester News*: Jonathan Barry, John Anyon, Simon Rogers, Emma Attwood, Jon Fuller-Rowell, Roy Booker, Rebecca Bourne and James Connell.

You can buy prints of any of the photographs in this book carrying a unique reference number. Log on to **www.worcesternews. co.uk/news/wnnewsphotosales** for details.

THE JUNE FLOOD

When the heavens opened on 24th June 2007, few expected what was to come in the next few days.

It seemed as if the rain would never stop. The most torrential downpours in more than 50 years soon put the county of Worcestershire on flood alert. Across the county, members of the Environment Agency assessed river levels and took decisions on if and when to raise flood barriers.

In Upton-upon-Severn they went up. In Worcester they didn't. The result was that Upton escaped the worst of the floods whilst Worcester was not so lucky. The result was a city under water.

Unfortunately, there was worse to come.

Left: River levels rising quickly in Upton-upon-Severn. 26076702.

Opposite page: Environment Agency staff in Hylton Road, Worcester. A decision was taken not to erect flood barriers here. 26078606.

Below: Environment Agency staff prepare Upton's flood defence system. 26076706.

Above: With Hylton Road in Worcester under water it was all hands to the pump to find alternative ways of getting the Worcester News *out. 26078604.*

Right: Flooded fields at Powick Bridge on the outskirts of Worcester. 26079403.

Opposite page: A cyclist makes his way along flooded Hylton Road in Worcester. 26078601.

UNDER WATER

The rivers Severn and Teme both burst their banks in the last week of June putting much of Worcester under water. Householders and businesses struggled to cope with the rising waters.

The *Worcester News* has its headquarters on Hylton Road in the city, a prime spot for flooding. With access to the offices impossible the only way of getting 18,500 newspapers out of the building and into the shops was for staff to form a human chain and carry them up a steep hill at the rear of the premises and into waiting delivery vans.

Meanwhile, the waters continued to rise.

FLOODED LANDMARKS

The June floods had a remarkable effect on the Worcestershire landscape. Rivers and surrounding fields became one, and mud and soil turned the water a dramatic colour.

Landmarks like the county cricket ground at New Road and Worcester's South Quay had the look of a rainy winter about them rather than what was supposed to be the height of summer.

For the cricket club this was the start of a devastating period that would see it made homeless and facing massive losses.

But at least the city's swans seemed to be enjoying themselves.

Left: The flooded scene at Worcester's South Quay. 26079404.

Below: The bloated River Severn through Worcester looked almost red as it filled with mud. 25070801.

Rain well and truly stopped play at Worcestershire's county cricket ground at New Road. 26077310.

You can buy prints of the photographs in this book if they have a unique reference number.
Log on to **www.worcesternews.co.uk/news/wnnewsphotosales** for details

9

WET, WET, WET

It really didn't matter where you looked in Worcester in the last week of June. There was water everywhere. The result of the equivalent of two months' rainfall in just 24 hours was plain to see.

Drinkers at the Talbot pub in Knightwick did not let the floods put them off their beer, however. Despite more than a foot of water lapping at the door of the pub, owner Annie Clift ferried staff to work and was ready to do the same for her customers.

'They can leave their cars outside the flood and I will ferry them in,' said Miss Clift: 'Canoes are welcome.'

Above: The scene outside the Talbot pub at Knightwick. Whatever the road sign says, there's water in every direction! 26076801.

Opposite page: The River Severn near to its June peak at Worcester Rowing Club. 26077903.

Left: A passer-by looks at the debris trapped under Worcester's New Road bridge. 26079402.

FUN FOR SOME

It was misery for most, but some people still managed to see the fun side of the June floods. From surfers in fields to schoolboys just enjoying being out and about in their wellies, there were those who made the most of things.

Warnings were issued to parents, however, about the dangers of letting their children play in and around flood waters. Aside from the risk of fast-moving rivers, there were also fears that the floods carried health risks due to the number of drains that had overflowed, washing sewage into the waters.

Above: Jack and Oliver Adams have a splashing time in the water. 26077225.

Right: Even intrepid Worcester News *reporters need help from time to time. Photographer Jon Fuller-Rowell carries reporter Rebecca Bourne through the floods.* 26078505.

Opposite page: Teenagers Rhys Coles and Ben Hardy trying to surf on a flooded field in Powick. 26078502.

Left: Craig Coleman, Cher Marston, Matthew Stephens and Kevin Marston wade through the flooded main street in Tenbury Wells. 26077212.

A TOWN UNDER WATER

Towns and villages across Worcestershire were awash as the June floods made their mark.

One of the worst hit was Tenbury Wells, when the River Teme burst its banks in the early hours of 26th June. More than 30 people were evacuated from their homes to the town's high school as homes and businesses bore the brunt of the deluge.

Many Tenbury residents had never seen flooding on such a scale. Bryan Pugh told the *Worcester News*: 'I have been here 37 years and I have never, ever seen a flood like this before.

Above: Tenbury was out of bounds unless you were a 4x4 driver. 26077227.

Left: A car tries to make its way through water from the Teme near Ham bridge, between Martley and Clifton-upon-Teme. 26077201.

NO ESCAPE FROM THE DELUGE

It didn't really matter who you were or what you were doing in Worcestershire during the summer of 2007 – you could not escape the floods.

Holidaymakers at a quiet caravan park in Upton-upon-Severn and residents of a permanent caravan site near Worcester were affected badly.

Meanwhile, farmers were beginning a summer of struggle that was about to be made worse by the foot-and-mouth outbreaks in Surrey. Livestock farmers were forced to bring their animals indoors while others saw crops destroyed by the floods.

Top: This permanent caravan park near Worcester was badly affected. 26077202.

Right: Farm hand Alan Critchlow stands in what should be a field of sweet corn at Holt Heath. 26079802.

Opposite page: Peaceful holidays were ruined as the floods struck at Pool House Caravan Park at Upton-upon-Severn. 26079401.

IT WASN'T JUST THE RAIN ...

The June floods brought more than just water into people's homes and businesses.

Many places saw sewage floating in the streets as the levels of rainfall overwhelmed drains.

Meanwhile, anything washed away from riverbanks, fields and streets ended up racing down swollen rivers. Debris piled up against many of the river bridges across the county, and there were fears that some would suffer structural damage.

Thankfully, all survived their unusual summer battering.

Left: Water surges against Teme Bridge in Tenbury, raising fears that the bridge could suffer damage. 26077215.

Opposite page: Locals inspect the mass of flood debris washed against Teme Bridge in Tenbury Wells. 26077221.

Below: The normally placid and picturesque Dick Brook, swollen by torrential rain at Prior Mill in Astley. 26075202.

THE CHAOS LEFT BEHIND

Once the torrential downpours had subsided, the damage nature had inflicted became clear for all to see.

In Shrawley and Astley there was devastation – homes were flooded out, possessions destroyed, roads blocked. Some people saw the contents of their gardens disappear into the raging floodwaters within a matter of minutes.

The clean-up operation was to last many weeks.

Top: The aftermath at a house in Shrawley. At one point, water was 12 ft deep in this home. 25070009.

Right: The scene of devastation in the front garden of Church Farm, Astley.

Opposite page: Garden furniture from the garden of Priors Mill, Astley, blocks the road.

Opposite page, left: Worcester racecourse became a fish graveyard once flood waters began to recede. 28090902

Opposite page, right: Wendy Wreghitt in the flooded kitchen of her home in Powick. 26078507.

Left: Farmer John Harper surveys destroyed sweet corn and spring barley crops on his land at Holt Heath. 26079801.

AS THE WATERS RECEDED

One of the most remarkable sights once floodwaters had receded was that of thousands of fish stranded on Worcester racecourse.

Environment Agency staff managed to return more than 10,000 fish to the Severn but many thousands perished on the badly-damaged racecourse. It was the first time in living memory that such an incident had occurred – yet it was to be repeated less than a month later.

Elsewhere, farmers began to assess the damage done to their crops while householders waited for insurance assessors to view their homes.

You can buy prints of the photographs in this book if they have a unique reference number.
Log on to www.worcesternews.co.uk/news/wnnewsphotosales for details

23

DRAMA JUST A MONTH LATER

The June floods were the worst summer floods to hit Worcestershire in living memory. Yet, within a month, much of the county was under water again as a 27-hour downpour brought with it even worse devastation.

Already sodden earth and swollen rivers simply could not take another freak rainstorm, and floods brought utter chaos to the county on 20th July.

Within hours of the downpour beginning, dramatic rescues were taking place in the centre of Worcester.

Right: Parents join the evacuation of children from the school. 29105506.

Far right: Head teacher Jeremy Harwood shows the strain as he plays a part in the rescue mission at Cherry Orchard Primary School. 29105516.

Opposite page: Firefighters carry children out of flooded Cherry Orchard Primary School in Worcester. 29105501.

THE RESCUES CONTINUE

Whilst police, firefighers, teachers and parents joined forces to carry youngsters from their flooded classrooms at Cherry Orchard Primary School in Worcester, a similar rescue mission was taking place at the nearby Timberdine Resource Centre.

At the resource centre many elderly and disabled people were ferried to safety by ambulance.

Left: A police officer helps during the rescue mission at Cherry Orchard Primary School. 29105513

Far left: A firefighter joins the evacuation of pupils from the school. 29105505.

Opposite page: Emergency services evacuate the elderly and disabled from the Timberdine Resource Centre in Worcester. 29106205.

You can buy prints of the photographs in this book if they have a unique reference number.
Log on to **www.worcesternews.co.uk/news/wnnewsphotosales** for details

27

Above left: Kasia Czyrko, aged three, from St Johns in Worcester, splashes through the flood at New Road. 29106711.

Opposite page: Crowds look at the floodwaters in New Road, Worcester. 29106709.

Above right: Pedestrians consider the best footwear for a wade across New Road. 29106712.

A TRIP TO SEE THE FLOODS

The morning after the night before brought hundreds of people out to see the floods in Worcester. With the torrential rain at an end, most people woke on the morning of 21st July to a watery landscape.

Many people in the Faithful City took a trip out to look at the floods. But, as the waters kept rising, it soon became clear that what was fun for some was utter misery for many others.

Above: Two wheels better than four. A cyclist pedals along Hylton Road. 29106713.

Right: Trying to stay dry. Shoppers at Homebase in Worcester taking no chances. 29105609.

TAKING A TRIP? IT WASN'T EASY

The depth of the floods in and around Worcester meant that even the smallest trip turned into a major expedition.

The city was virtually cut in two as the New Road bridge was closed. This meant that getting from the St Johns side of Worcester to the city centre was almost impossible.

Those who did attempt to get to the shops had few choices in terms of modes of transport.

Opposite page: A hardy soul wades waist-deep through the floodwater on Hylton Road in Worcester. 29106701.

LIFE HAS TO CARRY ON

Despite the once-in-a-lifetime floods in Worcester on the weekend of 21st and 22nd July, many aspects of normal life simply had to carry on. Whether it was shopping, visiting friends, taking the kids to various activities or – bizarrely enough – watering the plants, it simply had to be done.

The result was some odd sights in and around the city. And *Worcester News* photographers were there to capture them for posterity.

Right: Trolley splash. Shaun Miles and Yasmin Clews try a novel way of getting through the water. 29106730.

Far right:The flood outside the Severn View Hotel in Worcester might be ankle deep – but it doesn't reach the hanging baskets! 30108213.

Opposite page: Making a splash. A motorist battles along New Road in Worcester – putting pedestrians at risk of a soaking. 29106710.

You can buy prints of the photographs in this book if they have a unique reference number.
Log on to **www.worcesternews.co.uk/news/wnnewsphotosales** for details

33

DROITWICH IN THE FLOOD

Many businesses in Droitwich were severely damaged by the July floods. Water reached more than 10 ft high in the town's High Street, devastating many shops and offices.

When the waters receded they left raw sewage, rotting meat from a local butcher's and an entire pane of glass in their wake.

One trader, Viv Hudson, the managing director of Hotelshop UK, spoke to the *Worcester News* as she surveyed the damage.

She said: 'It's heartbreaking. It's taken eight years to build up the business.'

Above: Andrew Duggan up to his waist in the Droitwich flood waters. 29106507.

Above: Taped off for safety. Smoking electricity cables in the centre of Droitwich. 29106504

Opposite page: Crowds gather to look at Droitwich High Street under water. 29106506.

Right: How high was the flood? This toy fish appears to have been stranded after the waters receded. 30107806.

Far right: Kempsey vicar, Peter Holzapfel, suitably armed, on his way to a baptism. 30107805.

Opposite page: A driver makes his way through the village of Kempsey at the height of the floods. 30107803.

KEMPSEY IN THE FLOOD

It was only when routes out of Worcester were clear of water that the impact of the floods on the city's surrounding towns and villages became clear.

Large parts of the village of Kempsey were under water – but that did not stop a local vicar getting to a christening. The Rev Peter Holzapfel waded through the flood with a pop bottle filled with holy water and his robes in a carrier bag.

Another church in the nearby village of Norton hosted the baptism.

You can buy prints of the photographs in this book if they have a unique reference number.
Log on to **www.worcesternews.co.uk/news/wnnewsphotosales** for details

37

THE WORST FLOOD FOR SIXTY YEARS

The July flood was the worst disaster to hit the city since a similar deluge in 1947.

Many homes in Hylton Road were flooded as flood barriers again failed to be erected.

Unlike June, this time a decision was taken to erect the barriers – but the staff needed to do the work were stuck in huge tailbacks on the M5. When they eventually got to Worcester it was too late.

An Environment Agency spokesman said: 'Our officers were incredibly frustrated that despite a police escort they were not able to get the barriers where they were needed on time.'

Above: Flooded homes on Hylton Road in Worcester. 29106731.

Left: A couple survey the scene in Worcester city centre. 29106722.

Opposite page: Local people view the floods in Worcester city centre. 29106725.

Above: A river runs through it. The scene beneath the railway bridge on Hylton Road, Worcester. 29106728.

Right: This intrepid biker decides it's better to carry his wheels through the water. 29106726.

Opposite page: A lone cyclist makes his way through the floods in Worcester city centre. 29106720.

WAS THIS REALLY SUMMER?

Few people in Worcester could remember a summer flood as devastating as this July one. And hardly anyone could remember the River Severn in the city rising as fast as it did.

The result was a cityscape vastly different from the picturesque scenes usually associated with Worcester in the summer. The city's popular weather forecaster Paul Damari told the *Worcester News* at the time: 'I've never recorded rainfall like it in 50 years.'

More than five inches of rain fell on 20th July – the average rainfall for the whole of July is normally 1½ inches.

THERE'S A FRIDGE IN THE RIVER

Just as the floods in June filled fast-flowing rivers with debris of all kinds, so July brought more of the same.

There were some remarkable scenes. *Worcester News* photographer Emma Attwood captured a fridge racing down the River Avon at Pershore.

Elsewhere, plastic containers, tree branches and, memorably, a caravan were all spotted being borne on the current. The huge force of Worcestershire's swollen rivers meant that many structures, including the old bridge at Pershore, were cause for concern.

Above: Rubbish and plastic containers stuck in the River Severn in Worcester. 30108204.

Left: The force generated by the fast-flowing Avon led to engineers checking Pershore Old Bridge. 30108603.

Opposite page: A fridge races under Pershore Bridge, swept along the swollen River Avon. 30108606.

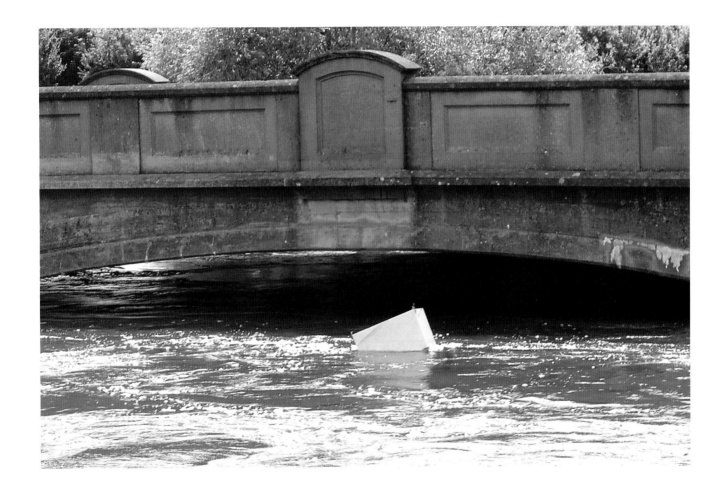

HELL ON THE ROADS

The weekend of the July floods brought Worcestershire's transport network to a halt.

Thousands of motorists were stranded on the M5 and M50 on the night of 20th July, with many forced to sleep in their cars.

Some drivers saw their cars written off after getting trapped by the rising waters. Rescue organisations like the AA and RAC reported the busiest night in their histories.

Rail lines were closed and bus services cancelled. The roads that escaped the worst of the flooding became clogged as drivers sought alternative routes.

Above: Cars struggle to negotiate Barbourne Road in Worcester. 29105604.

Right: Trying to get through. Even this AA van had trouble on routes like the A4133 between Ombersley and Droitwich. 29105801.

Opposite page: The sign says it all. Roads across the county were closed as a result of the floods. 29106717.

IT'S JUST NOT CRICKET

The July floods effectively made Worcestershire County Cricket Club homeless.

Just weeks after clearing up in the wake of the June deluge, the New Road pitch was again under feet of water.

The result was no more cricket at New Road and the team was forced to play at venues like Kidderminster. It is estimated the club lost £500,000 as a result.

Despite relegation from the First Division of the County Championship, the season did at least end on a high as the club clinched the Pro40 title.

Right: Advertising hoardings lie strewn across the flooded outfield at New Road. 29106715.

Far right: How do we get out? Kitchen staff at New Road survey the damage. 29106719.

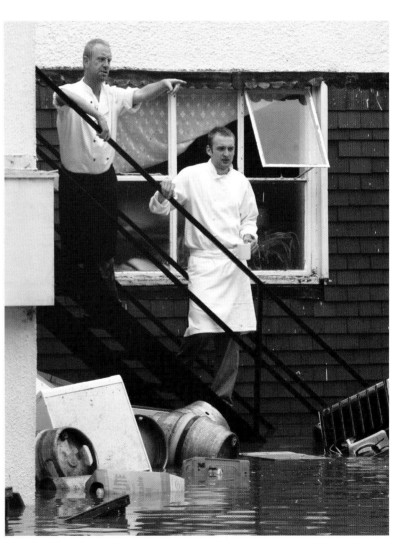

Opposite page: What a mess. Seats and fencing float across the New Road cricket pitch. 29106708.

Opposite page: Worcester racecourse under water. The photograph was taken on 24th July. Needless to say, the next day's meeting did not go ahead. 30108209.

Left: Rain well and truly stopped play at the Kings School cricket ground in Worcester. 29106705.

Below: Upton Sports Club was ready for the new rugby season – unfortunately its pitches were more suited to water sports. 30109002.

BAD SUMMER FOR SPORT

It wasn't just Worcestershire's cricketers who suffered during the floods. At Worcester racecourse, the damage caused to the track by two major floods meant that all racing was abandoned for the remainder of 2007.

As with their cricketing counterparts, racecourse bosses at Pitchcroft found themselves totting up losses of hundreds of thousands of pounds.

Rugby, football and cricket clubs across the county saw their pitches become lakes and then faced a major battle to save their seasons once the waters had receded.

Above: Firefighters inside the flooded reception area at Timberdine Resource Centre in Worcester. 29106202.

Above right: A common sight. Sandbags and discarded furniture in New Street, Upton-upon-Severn. 30109001.

Opposite page: Heroes in a dinghy. Tom Wells and Colin Phillips rescued a dozen residents and their pets from flooded homes at Callow End. 30107809.

ASSESSING THE DAMAGE

In the days that followed the 20th of July floods, people began assessing the damage the waters had caused and tales of heroism were slowly revealed.

Stories came to light of people who displayed amazing selflessness on the night of the flood, rescuing people and opening up their homes to those who had been flooded out.

When the waters receded, however, the true cost of the floods could be seen.

The Prince of Wales and the Duchess of Cornwall visit a damaged pub during a visit to Upton-upon-Severn. 30107501.

Above: Conservative Party Leader David Cameron talks to firefighters involved in the floods rescue operation at Upton-upon-Severn. 30110403.

Right: Environment Secretary Hilary Benn (second from right) views the Worcester floods from the city's New Road bridge. 29106801.

VIPS VIEW THE DAMAGE

As the floods in Worcestershire made national news headlines, an increasing number of politicians and other dignitaries arrived in the county to view the devastation for themselves.

Upton-upon-Severn was a popular destination for the VIPs. The Prince of Wales and the Duchess of Cornwall put a smile on local faces as they toured the town. Conservative leader David Cameron also visited, talking to emergency services and local farmers.

Meanwhile Environment Secretary Hilary Benn visited Worcester to see the extent of the flooding in the city and to hear about the issues associated with the non-erection of flood defences on Hylton Road.

THE BIG CLEAN-UP: WORCESTER AND DROITWICH

Once the waters had receded, scenes of utter devastation were revealed across the county.

Homes and businesses were wrecked, with many people facing months of misery before they could live in their houses again. For businesses it was a battle to protect livelihoods.

As the big clean-up began in earnest, *Worcester News* photographers were on hand to record the human cost of the worst floods in living memory.

Above: Brushes and carpets signal the start of the clean-up in Worcester's Hylton Road. 30108401.

Left: Washing away the debris. Council staff get to work in Worcester city centre. 30108208.

Opposite page: Household furniture lying outside in Hunters Way, Droitwich, in the aftermath of the floods. 30107307.

THE BIG CLEAN-UP: UPTON AND KEMPSEY

The towns and villages around Worcester began a massive clean-up operation once rivers had returned to their usual levels.

Upton-upon-Severn, used to floods, fought back in impressive style. Pubs opened as quickly as they could and the town staged a series of festivals aimed at ensuring visitors to the picturesque riverside venue knew that Upton was back in business.

There was still much work to be done but townsfolk attacked it in stoic fashion and with a smile on their faces.

Left: Jonathan Butler and Kate Hardings, owners of Ye Olde Anchor Inn in Upton-upon-Severn, in their flood-damaged bar. 30109004.

Far left: The devastated kitchen of the Star Inn at Upton. 30109007.

Opposite page: Sodden carpets and other household items stripped out of homes in Kempsey. 30107804.

DROITWICH HIGH STREET

The floods had a huge impact on the High Street in Droitwich. The town's central commercial area was closed to traffic for more than a week as a huge operation to get the street clean took place.

Some shops saw up to 10 ft of water pour into their premises. Around 40 animals died in the town's pet shop, while a local butcher lost more than £3,000 in stock.

Two months after the flood newsagent Ron Patel was still operating from a van outside his shop. But spirits among the town traders remained high. Mr Patel told the *Worcester News*: 'We may be withered, we may be wilted but we are definitely not beaten.'

Right: Pet shop owner, Les Bowl, shows the level flood waters reached in his Droitwich store. 30109104.

Far right: The operation to clean away mud and sewage from Droitwich High Street. 30107305.

Opposite page: Council workers clear away flood-damaged items in Droitwich High Street. 30109101.

THE POWER OF THE FLOOD

Many businesses in the Faithful City suffered huge losses during the July flood.

One used car dealer saw 30 of his cars destroyed as a 'tsunami' struck his premises.

Peter Smith, managing director of Bromyard Road Motors, said £50,000 of damage was caused after the force of the water demolished a brick wall.

He described the scene to the *Worcester News*: 'The cars had been swept towards the wall – some had turned round completely in the water. It seemed as if they were dancing in the rain.'

Other motor dealers reported similar problems with damage estimated at hundreds of thousands of pounds.

Left: Children cycle along mud-strewn pavements in the centre of Worcester after the floodwaters had receded. 30108205.

Left: A sofa washed onto Hylton Road in Worcester. 30108214.

Opposite page: The devastation caused by the floods at Bromyard Road Motors in Worcester. 30109505.

SO MUCH TO DO

Cherry Orchard Primary School was a scene of drama on the afternoon of 20th June as emergency services, parents and teachers struggled to evacuate pupils from their flooded classrooms on the last day of term, as previously detailed in this book.

Just five days later head teacher Jeremy Harwood, who had coordinated the rescue of his 550 pupils, was back at the school assessing the damage.

He arrived to find parents already on site ripping out damaged carpets. 'It was just fantastic to see,' said Mr Harwood.

Above: Laughern Brook under Bromyard Road in Worcester after the flood had receded. 30109506.

Right: One man and his brush. Cleaning up after the floods in Hylton Road, Worcester. 30108211.

Opposite page: Cherry Orchard Primary School head teacher Jeremy Harwood begins his summer holidays assessing the damage caused to his Worcester school. 30109507.

COULD IT HAPPEN AGAIN?

And after the floods all that was left for the people of Worcester to do was to clean up and plan for the future. The big question for many residents of the city and its surrounding towns and villages was whether the summer floods were a once-in-a-lifetime incident or a sign of things to come.

Some experts believe that climate change makes a repetition of the events of June and July 2007 inevitable. If that is the case, then serious thought needs to be given to where houses are built in the future. Plans are already in place for a permanent flood barrier in Worcester.

The summer floods of 2007 will live long in the memory. Let us hope that it will be many years before Worcestershire is under water again during the summer months.

Top Left: Washing away the flood debris in Hylton Road, Worcester. 30108402.

Lower left: Hosing down a flood-hit car park in the city centre. 30108207.

Right: A resident battles to clear flood water from his house in Barbourne Road, Worcester. 29105608.